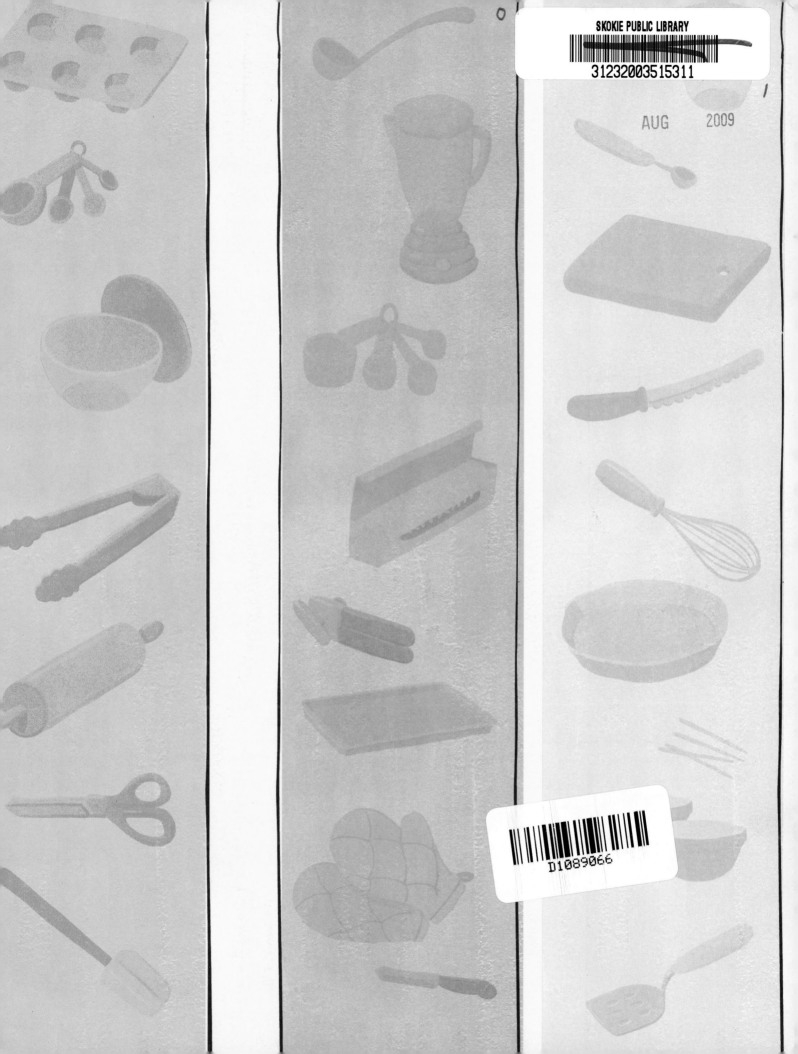

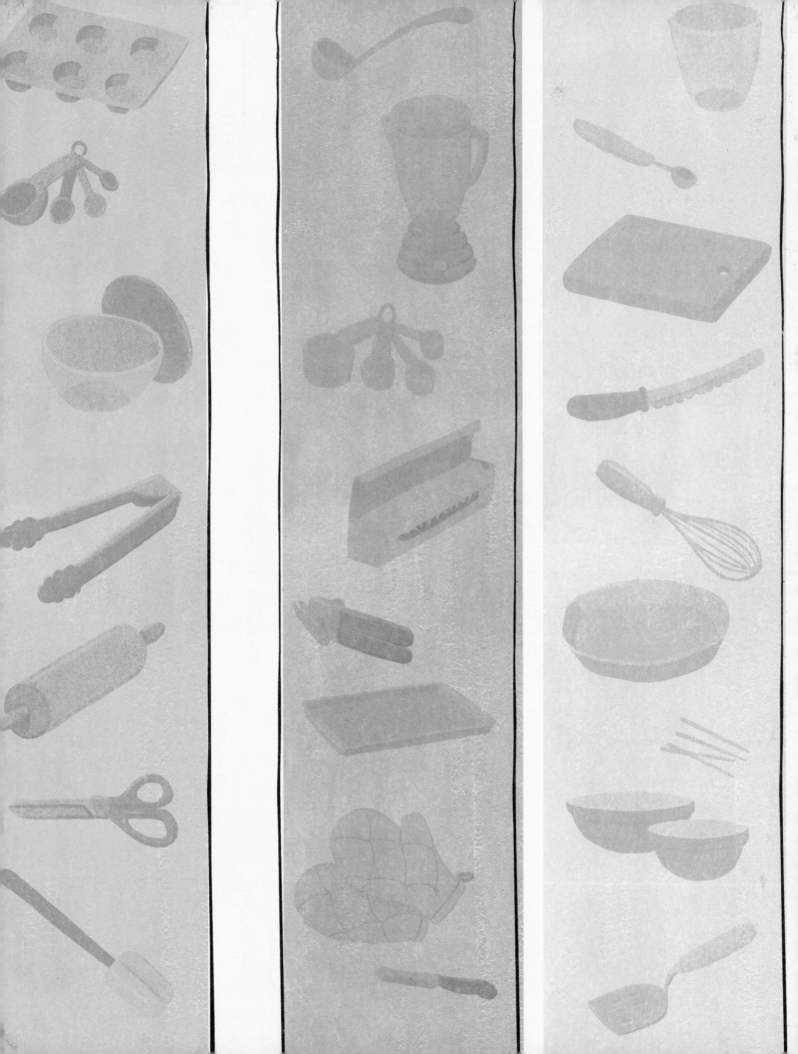

Chocolate Chill-out Cake

and Other Yummy Desserts

by Nick Fauchald   illustrated by Rick Peterson

Special thanks to our content adviser:
Joanne L. Slavin, Ph.D., R.D.
Professor of Food Science and Nutrition
University of Minnesota

PICTURE WINDOW BOOKS
Minneapolis, Minnesota

Editors: Christianne Jones and Carol Jones
Designer: Tracy Davies
Page Production: Melissa Kes

Art Director: Nathan Gassman
The illustrations in this book were created with acrylics and gouache.

Picture Window Books
151 Good Counsel Drive
P.O. Box 669
Mankato, MN 56002-0669
877-845-55416
www.picturewindowbooks.com

The illustration on page 5 is from *www.mypyramid.gov*.

Printed in the United States of America

All books published by Picture Window Books are manufactured
with paper containing at least 10 percent post-consumer waste.

Library of Congress Cataloging-in-Publication Data
Fauchald, Nick.
Chocolate Chill-out Cake: and other yummy desserts / by Nick Fauchald ; illustrated by Rick Peterson.
p. cm. — (Kids dish)
Includes index.
ISBN-13: 978-1-4048-3997-7 (library binding)
1. Desserts—Juvenile literature. I. Peterson, Rick. II. Title.
TX773.F3345 2008
641.8'6–dc22   2007032925

Editors' note: The author based the difficulty levels of the recipes on the skills and time required, as well as the number of ingredients and tools needed. Adult help and supervision is required for all recipes.

Table of Contents

EASY

INTERMEDIATE

ADVANCED

Nick Fauchald is the author of many children's books. After attending the French Culinary School in Manhattan, he helped launch the magazine *Every Day with Rachael Ray*. He is currently an editor at *Food & Wine* magazine and lives in New York City. Although Nick has worked with some of the world's best chefs, he still thinks kids are the most fun and creative cooks to work with.

Dear Kids,

There's no better way to end a great meal than with a delicious dessert. Dessert can even be healthy! Many of the recipes in this cookbook are good for you, and you can make them with only a little help from an adult.

Cooking is fun, and safety in the kitchen is very important. As you begin your cooking adventure, please remember these tips:

★ Make sure an adult is in the kitchen with you.
★ Tie back your hair and tuck in all loose clothing.
★ Read the recipe from start to finish before you begin.
★ Wash your hands before you start and whenever they get messy.
★ Wash all fresh fruits and vegetables.
★ Take your time cutting the ingredients.
★ Use oven mitts whenever you are working with hot foods or equipment.
★ Stay in the kitchen the entire time you are cooking.
★ Clean up when you are finished.

Now, choose a recipe that sounds tasty, check with an adult, and get cooking. Your friends and family are hungry!

Enjoy,
Nick

KIDS DISH

Note to Adults:

Learning to cook is an exciting, challenging adventure for young people. It helps kids build confidence, learn responsibility, become familiar with food and nutrition, practice math, science, and motor skills, and follow directions. Here are some ways you can help kids get the most out of their cooking experiences:

• Encourage them to read the entire recipe before they begin cooking. Make sure they have everything they need and understand all of the steps.

• Make sure young cooks have a kid-friendly workspace. If your kitchen counter is too high for them, offer them a stepstool or a table to work at.

• Expect new cooks to make a little mess, and encourage them to clean it up when they are finished.

• Help multiple cooks divide the tasks before they begin.

• Enjoy what the kids just cooked together.

MyPyramid

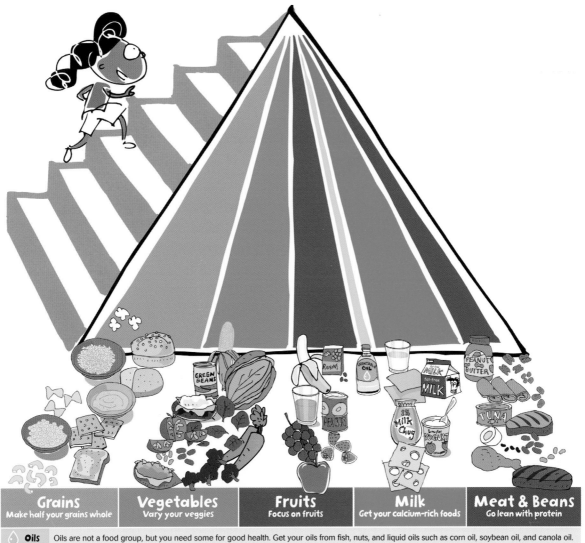

Grains	Vegetables	Fruits	Milk	Meat & Beans
Make half your grains whole	Vary your veggies	Focus on fruits	Get your calcium-rich foods	Go lean with protein

◊ **Oils** Oils are not a food group, but you need some for good health. Get your oils from fish, nuts, and liquid oils such as corn oil, soybean oil, and canola oil.

In 2005, the U.S. government created MyPyramid, a plan for healthy eating and living. The new MyPyramid plan contains 12 separate diet plans based on your age, gender, and activity level. For more information about MyPyramid, visit *www.mypyramid.gov.*

The pyramid at the top of each recipe shows the main food groups included. Use the index to find recipes that include food from the food group of your choice, major ingredients used, recipe levels, and appliances/equipment needed.

Special Tips and Glossary

Cracking Eggs: Tap the egg on the counter until it cracks. Hold the egg over a small bowl. Gently pull the two halves of the shell apart until the contents fall into the bowl.

Measuring Dry Ingredients: Measure dry ingredients (such as flour and sugar) by spooning the ingredient into a measuring cup until it's full. Then level off the top of the cup with the back of a butter knife.

Measuring Wet Ingredients: Place a clear measuring cup on a flat surface, then pour the liquid into the cup until it reaches the correct measuring line. Be sure to check the liquid at eye level.

Bake: cook food in an oven

Cool: set hot food on a wire rack until it's no longer hot

Cover: put container lid, plastic wrap, or aluminum foil over a food; use aluminum foil if you're baking the food, and plastic wrap if you're chilling, freezing, microwaving, or leaving it on the counter

Drain: pour off a liquid, leaving food behind; usually done with a strainer or colander

Grease: spread butter, cooking spray, or shortening on a piece of cookware so food doesn't stick

Melt: heat a solid (such as butter) until it becomes a liquid

Preheat: turn an oven on before you use it; it usually takes about 15 minutes to preheat an oven

Slice: cut something into thin pieces

Sprinkle: to scatter something in small bits

Stir: mix ingredients with a spoon until blended or combined

Whisk: stir a mixture rapidly until it's smooth

METRIC CONVERSION CHART

1/8 teaspoon (0.5 milliliter)
1/4 teaspoon (1 milliliter)
1/2 teaspoon (2.5 milliliters)
1 teaspoon (5 milliliters)
1 1/2 teaspoons (7.5 milliliters)

1 tablespoon (15 milliliters)
2 tablespoons (30 milliliters)
3 tablespoons (45 milliliters)
4 tablespoons (60 milliliters)

1/4 cup (60 milliliters)
1/3 cup (75 milliliters)
1/2 cup (125 milliliters)
3/4 cup (180 milliliters)
1 cup (250 milliliters)
1 1/4 cups (300 milliliters)
1 1/2 cups (375 milliliters)
2 cups (500 milliliters)
2 1/2 cups (625 milliliters)
3 cups (750 milliliters)
4 cups (950 milliliters)

5 ounces (140 grams)
8 ounces (224 grams)
12 ounces (336 grams)
14 ounces (392 grams)
16 ounces (448 grams)

TEMPERATURE CONVERSION CHART

350° Fahrenheit (175° Celsius)
375° Fahrenheit (190° Celsius)
400° Fahrenheit (200° Celsius)

Kitchen Tools

HERE ARE THE TOOLS YOU'LL USE WHEN COOKING THE RECIPES IN THIS BOOK ★

8-by-8-inch baking pan

9-by-13-inch baking pan

Aluminum foil

Baking sheet

Blender

Cooking spray

Can opener

Cheese grater

Cooling rack

Cutting board

Fork

Glasses

Glass pie dish

Large glass bowl

Measuring cups

Measuring spoons

Metal spatula

Microwave-safe bowls

Mixing bowls

Oven mitts

Paper cups

Paper towels

Plastic wrap

Plastic bags

Rolling pin

Rubber spatula

Serrated knife

Small bowl

Small, sharp knife

Toothpicks

Spoon

Whisk

Wooden craft sticks

Wooden spoon

7

This recipe includes

FRUITS, MILK

Orange Creamsicle Slush

INGREDIENTS

2 cups orange juice
1/2 cup sugar
3 tablespoons lemon juice
1/4 cup vanilla yogurt

TOOLS

Measuring cups
Measuring spoons
Medium mixing bowl
Whisk
9-by-13-inch metal
     baking pan
Oven mitts
Fork
Spoon
Small bowls

NUTRITION NOTE★

Orange juice is high in
vitamin C, which helps
your body fight illness.

Combine the orange juice, sugar, and lemon juice in a medium mixing bowl. Whisk. Let the mixture stand for 10 minutes. Whisk again.

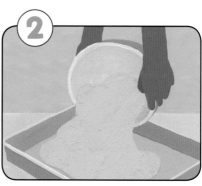

Pour mixture into the baking pan. Freeze for 30 minutes.

Use oven mitts to remove the pan from the freezer.

Add the yogurt to the frozen juice, stir with a fork until blended, and return the mixture to the freezer.

5 Every 15 minutes, remove the mixture from the freezer and stir with a fork until the mixture becomes slushy. [NOTE: This takes about 45 minutes more.]

6 Spoon the slushy mixture into bowls and serve.

This Recipe Includes
MILK

Chocolate Chill-Out Cake

INGREDIENTS

16 mini ice-cream
   sandwiches
1/2 cup chocolate syrup
1 container whipped
   topping, 8-ounces
1 chocolate bar, frozen

TOOLS

9-by-13-inch baking pan
Measuring cups
Rubber spatula
Cheese grater
Plastic wrap
Oven mitts
Small, sharp knife

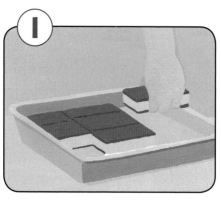

1

Line the bottom of the baking pan with a layer of ice-cream sandwiches.

2

Pour the chocolate syrup on top of the ice-cream sandwiches.

3

Using a rubber spatula, spread the whipped topping on top of the chocolate syrup.

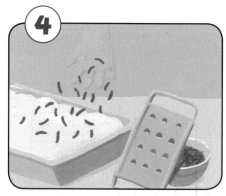

4

Ask an adult to grate the chocolate bar with a cheese grater. Sprinkle the grated chocolate over the whipped topping.

5

Cover the cake with plastic wrap and place in the freezer for 1 hour.

6 Slice into 16 pieces and serve.

This Recipe Includes
FRUITS, MILK

Yogurt on a Stick

INGREDIENTS
1 cup plain low-fat yogurt
1 cup fresh or thawed
   frozen strawberries
2 tablespoons honey

TOOLS
Measuring cups
Measuring spoons
Blender
4 paper cups, 5-ounces each
Aluminum foil
4 small, wooden craft sticks
   or plastic spoons

1. Place the yogurt, fruit, and honey in a blender. Cover and blend for 15 seconds or until smooth.

2. Pour the mixture into paper cups, filling them about three-quarters full.

3. Cover the cups with small squares of aluminum foil.

4. Poke the wooden sticks through the center of the foil covers, standing the sticks up straight.

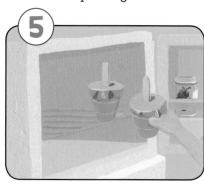

5. Place the cups on a level surface in the freezer for about 5 hours or until frozen.

FUN WITH FOOD★ Use your favorite fruits and flavored yogurt to make your own flavor.

6. Peel off the foil and paper cups and serve.

Black-and-White Malts

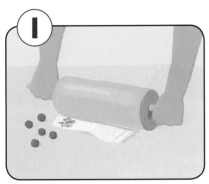

1 Pour the malted milk balls into a plastic bag, press out air, and seal. Use a rolling pin to break the balls into little pieces.

2 Put the ice cream and milk into the blender. Cover and blend the mixture for 15 seconds or until combined.

3 Pour the malt into two glasses.

4 Sprinkle the crushed malted milk balls on the top and serve. [NOTE: If the malts are runny, put them in the freezer for 10 minutes or until firm.]

FUN WITH FOOD★ Crush your favorite candy bars and use instead of the malted milk balls. You can also mix in other flavors of ice cream, such as strawberry or cherry.

INGREDIENTS

1/3 cup chocolate covered malted milk balls
1 cup vanilla ice cream
1 cup chocolate ice cream
1/2 cup milk

TOOLS

Measuring cups
Plastic bag
Rolling pin
Blender
Glasses

13

This Recipe Includes

FRUITS, MILK, GRAINS

Three-Berry Trifle

INGREDIENTS

1 pound cake, 16-ounces
1 package frozen blueberries,
    12-ounces
1 package frozen raspberries,
    12-ounces
1 package frozen blackberries,
    12-ounces
1 can sweetened condensed
    milk, 14-ounces
1 package instant vanilla
    pudding mix, 5-ounces
1/2 cup milk
1 container whipped topping,
    8-ounces

TOOLS

Serrated knife
Cutting board
Large glass bowl
Measuring cups
Can opener
Large mixing bowl
Rubber spatula
Spoon
Plastic wrap

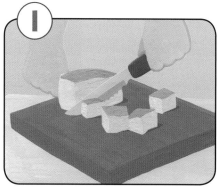

Ask an adult to cut the pound cake into cubes.

Arrange half of the cake cubes in the bottom of a large glass bowl.

Spread half of the blueberries, raspberries, and blackberries on top of the cake. Add another layer of the remaining cake cubes and top with the remaining berries.

Open the can of sweetened condensed milk.

Place the pudding mix, milk, sweetened condensed milk, and one-half of the whipped topping in a large mixing bowl and stir with a rubber spatula.

Spread the pudding mixture over the berries. Top with the remaining whipped topping.

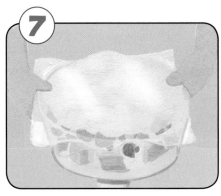

Cover the trifle with plastic wrap and refrigerate 2 hours.

8 Spoon into small dishes to serve.

This Recipe Includes
FRUITS, GRAINS

Blueberry Crumble Bars

INGREDIENTS

3 cups all-purpose flour
1 teaspoon baking powder
1/4 teaspoon salt
1 1/2 cups sugar
1 cup softened butter
1 large egg
1 tablespoon cornstarch
4 cups fresh blueberries

TOOLS

9-by-13-inch baking pan
Cooking spray
2 medium mixing bowls
Measuring cups
Measuring spoons
Wooden spoon
Fork
Oven mitts
Small, sharp knife

1

Preheat the oven to 400°.

2

Spray the baking pan with cooking spray.

3

Pour the flour, baking powder, salt, and 1 cup of the sugar into a medium mixing bowl and stir.

4

Add the butter and egg and stir with a fork until the dough is crumbly.

5

Spoon half of the dough into the prepared pan and press evenly to cover the bottom of the pan.

NUTRITION NOTE★ Fruits and vegetables are a major source of vitamins A and C. These vitamins are loaded with antioxidants, which help fight disease.

6 Pour the cornstarch, blueberries, and the remaining sugar into another medium mixing bowl. Stir until the berries are coated.

7 Spread the blueberry mixture evenly over the crust.

8 Sprinkle the remaining dough over the blueberries.

9 Ask an adult to bake the bars for 45 minutes or until lightly browned and bubbly. Let cool for 20 minutes.

IO Cut into 16 squares and serve.

This Recipe Includes

GRAINS

Apple Cinnamon Granola Cookies

INGREDiENTS

1 cup all-purpose flour
1/2 teaspoon baking soda
1/2 teaspoon salt
1/2 cup unsalted
    softened butter
3/4 cup firmly packed
    brown sugar
1 large egg
1/2 teaspoon pure
    vanilla extract
1 1/2 cups apple
    cinnamon granola

TOOLS

Measuring cups
Measuring spoons
Medium mixing bowl
Large mixing bowl
Wooden spoon
Cooking spray
2 baking sheets
Oven mitts
Metal spatula
Wire cooling rack

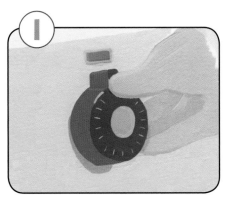

Preheat the oven to 350°.

Pour the flour, baking soda, and salt into a medium mixing bowl and stir.

Combine the butter and sugar in a large mixing bowl. Beat together with a wooden spoon.

Add the egg and vanilla to the butter mixture and beat again.

18

Pour the flour mixture and granola into the butter mixture and stir.

Grease the baking sheets and drop the cookie dough by the rounded tablespoonful about 2 inches apart.

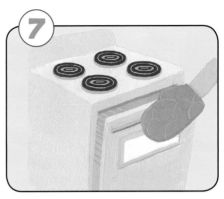

Ask an adult to bake the cookies for 12 to 15 minutes or until golden brown. Transfer the cookies from the baking sheet to a wire rack using a metal spatula.

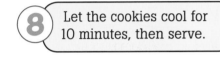

Let the cookies cool for 10 minutes, then serve.

CooKieS

This Recipe Includes
MILK, GRAINS

Chillin' Cheesecake

INGREDIENTS

7 cinnamon graham
  crackers
4 tablespoons
  unsalted butter
2 packages softened cream
  cheese (8 ounces each)
3 tablespoons lemon juice
1/2 teaspoon pure
  vanilla extract
1 can sweetened condensed
  milk, 14-ounces
1 cup fresh berries for
  topping (optional)

TOOLS

Large, resealable plastic bag
Rolling pin
Measuring spoons
Measuring cups
Medium microwave-safe
  bowl
Wooden spoon
Glass pie dish
Oven mitts
Medium mixing bowl
Can opener
Rubber spatula
Small, sharp knife

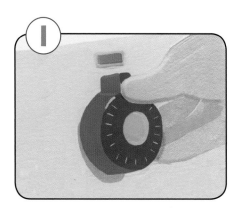
Preheat the oven to 350°.

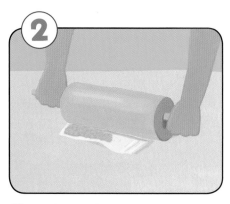
Place the graham crackers in a large resealable plastic bag, press out all of the air, and seal. Roll over the crackers with a rolling pin to crush them into crumbs.

Place the butter in a medium microwave-safe bowl. Ask an adult to heat the butter in the microwave for 60 seconds or until melted. Add the graham cracker crumbs to the butter and stir with the wooden spoon until combined.

Press the mixture into a glass pie dish to form a crust on the bottom and up the sides. Ask an adult to bake the pie crust for 7 minutes or until firm. Let cool completely (about 30 minutes).

Place cream cheese, lemon juice, and vanilla extract into a medium mixing bowl and beat with a wooden spoon until smooth (about 2 minutes).

Add the sweetened condensed milk to the cream cheese and beat again until smooth (about 2 minutes more).

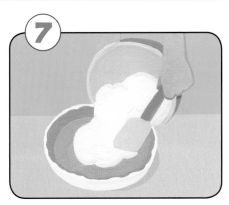

Pour the filling into the cooled pie crust and spread evenly with the rubber spatula. Place the pie in the refrigerator until chilled (about 3 hours).

8 Cut the pie into wedges and serve with berry topping, if desired.

This Recipe Includes
FRUIT, MILK, GRAINS

Banana Bread Pudding

INGREDIENTS

1 ripe banana
1 large egg
1/2 cup applesauce
1/4 cup milk
2 tablespoons honey
1 tablespoon brown sugar
1 teaspoon ground cinnamon
1/4 teaspoon ground nutmeg
1/2 cup raisins
2 1/2 cups plain
    bread crumbs

TOOLS

8-by-8-inch baking pan
Cooking spray
Large mixing bowl
Fork
Measuring cups
Measuring spoons
Wooden spoon
Oven mitts

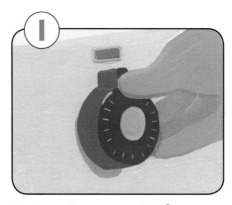

Preheat the oven to 350°.

Spray the baking pan with cooking spray.

Peel the banana and place it a large mixing bowl. Smash the banana with a fork until mushy.

Add the egg, applesauce, milk, and honey to the bowl with the banana and stir until combined.

22

NUTRITION NOTE★ Bananas are high in potassium, which helps your muscles and nerves work their best.

Add the brown sugar, cinnamon, nutmeg, raisins, and bread crumbs to the egg mixture and stir.

Press the mixture into the baking pan to cover the bottom.

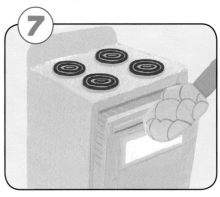

Ask an adult to bake the pudding for 30 minutes or until set. Let cool 10 minutes.

8 Cut and serve.

This Recipe Includes
FRUITS, GRAINS

Chocolate Cherry Cake

INGREDIENTS

1 1/4 cups all-purpose flour
1/3 cup unsweetened
    cocoa powder
1 1/2 teaspoons
    baking soda
1/8 teaspoon salt
1 cup dried cherries
1/2 cup softened butter
1 cup sugar
1 large egg
1 cup milk
1 teaspoon pure
    vanilla extract
1 teaspoon balsamic
    vinegar

TOOLS

8-by-8-inch baking pan
Cooking spray
Measuring cups
Measuring spoons
Medium mixing bowl
Wooden spoon
Large mixing bowl
Fork
Rubber spatula
Oven mitts
Toothpick
Wire cooling rack
Small, sharp knife

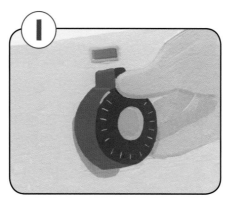

Preheat the oven to 350°.

Grease the baking pan with cooking spray.

Pour the flour, cocoa powder, baking soda, salt, and cherries into a medium mixing bowl and stir.

Put the butter and sugar in a large mixing bowl and mash with a fork until combined.

5

Add the egg, milk, vanilla, and balsamic vinegar to the butter and sugar mix and stir until no big lumps remain.

6

A little at a time, add the flour into the egg mixture and stir with a rubber spatula until smooth.

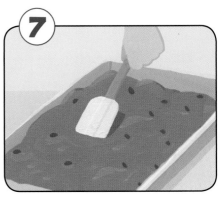

7

Scrape the batter into the pan and spread evenly with a rubber spatula.

8

Ask an adult to bake the cake for 40 minutes, or until a toothpick inserted into the center comes out clean. Set the cake on a rack to cool for 30 minutes.

9 Cut the cake and serve.

FRUITS, GRAINS

Applesauce Cake

INGREDIENTS
1 teaspoon baking soda
1 tablespoon warm water
1 cup applesauce
1 cup sugar
1/2 cup softened butter
1 teaspoon ground
  cinnamon
1 teaspoon pure
  vanilla extract
1 cup raisins
2 cups flour

TOOLS
9-by-13-inch baking pan
Cooking spray
Measuring spoons
Small bowl
Wooden spoon
Measuring cups
Large bowl
Oven mitts
Wire cooling rack

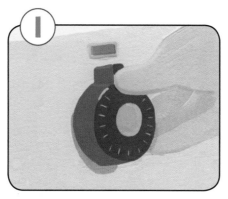

Preheat the oven to 375°.

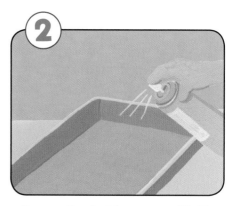

Grease the baking pan with the cooking spray.

Put the baking soda and water in a small mixing bowl, stir, and let sit until the soda is dissolved.

Place the applesauce, sugar, butter, dissolved baking soda mixture, cinnamon, vanilla extract, and raisins into a large mixing bowl and stir.

26

HEALTHY CHOICE★ When buying applesauce, look for "pure" or "unsweetened" on the label, which means it doesn't contain added sugar.

Add in the flour and stir until combined.

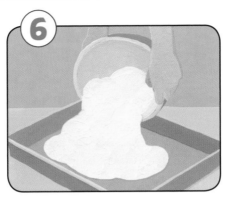

Pour the batter into the baking pan.

Ask an adult to bake the cake for 35 minutes or until golden. Let cool completely on a wire cooling rack.

8 Cut and serve.

This Recipe Includes
FRUITS, GRAINS

Cherry Crisp

INGREDIENTS

4 tablespoons softened butter
1/4 cup brown sugar
1/2 teaspoon ground
   cinnamon
1/8 teaspoon salt
1/2 cup oats
1/2 cup plus 1 tablespoon
   all-purpose flour
1/2 cup chopped pecans,
   optional
1 bag frozen cherries,
   thawed (14 ounces)
1 teaspoon vanilla extract
1/2 cup granulated sugar
Whipped cream for serving,
   optional

TOOLS

Measuring spoons
Measuring cups
2 Medium mixing bowls
Fork
8-by-8-inch baking pan
Cooking spray
Oven mitts

For the topping, put the butter, brown sugar, cinnamon, and salt into a medium mixing bowl and mash with a fork until blended.

Stir in the oats, 1/2 cup of the flour, and the pecans. Place the topping in the refrigerator while you make the cherry filling.

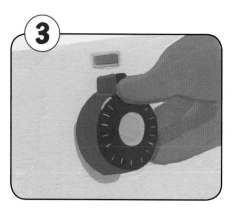

Preheat the oven to 375°.

Grease the baking pan with the cooking spray.

28

5

Put the cherries and vanilla extract in a medium mixing bowl and stir. Add the sugar and the remaining flour and stir gently until the cherries are coated.

6

Pour the cherry filling into the baking dish and spread evenly over the bottom.

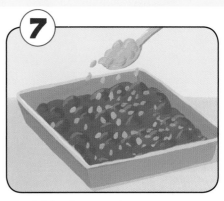

7

Sprinkle the topping over the cherries.

8

Ask an adult to bake the crisp for 30 minutes or until the topping is brown and filling is bubbling. Let cool for 20 minutes.

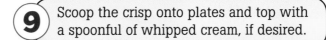

9 Scoop the crisp onto plates and top with a spoonful of whipped cream, if desired.

FRUITS

This Recipe Includes

Pear Cobbler

INGREDIENTS
3 tablespoons butter
2 cans of pear halves
1 cup all-purpose flour
1 cup granulated sugar
1 teaspoon baking powder
1/2 teaspoon salt
1/4 cup milk
1/4 cup apple juice
1 teaspoon pure
   vanilla extract
2 tablespoons brown sugar
Whipped cream for serving,
   optional

TOOLS
Small microwave-safe bowl
9-by-13-inch baking pan
Can opener
Paper towels
Measuring cups
Measuring spoons
Medium mixing bowl
Wooden spoon
Rubber spatula
Small mixing bowl
Spoon
Oven mitts

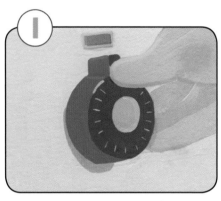

Preheat the oven to 400°.

Place the butter in a small microwave-safe bowl. Ask an adult to heat the butter in the microwave for 60 seconds or until melted. Pour half of the melted butter on the bottom of the baking pan.

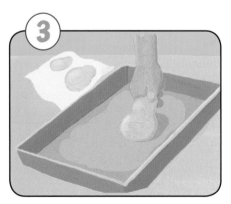

Open the pears and drain the pear halves on a paper towel. Arrange the pear halves in rows over the butter. [NOTE: The cut side of the pears should be down.]

Put the flour, 1/2 cup of the granulated sugar, the baking powder, and salt in a medium mixing bowl and stir.

30

Add the remaining melted butter, milk, apple juice, and vanilla extract and stir with a rubber spatula until combined.

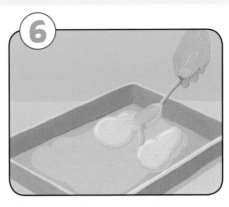

Spoon the batter over the pear halves, making sure that each pear is covered with some of the batter.

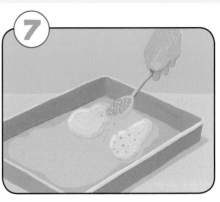

Combine the remaining sugar and the brown sugar in a small mixing bowl and stir. Sprinkle over the pear halves.

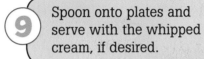

Spoon onto plates and serve with the whipped cream, if desired.

Ask an adult to bake the cobbler for 45 minutes or until the topping is golden brown and cooked through. Let cool for 10 minutes.

INDEX

ON THE WEB

FactHound offers a safe, fun way to find Web sites related to topics in this book. All of the sites on FactHound have been researched by our staff.

1.   Visit *www.facthound.com*
2.   Type in this special code: 1404839976
3.   Click on the FETCH IT button.

Your trusty FactHound will fetch the best sites for you!

KIDS DISH

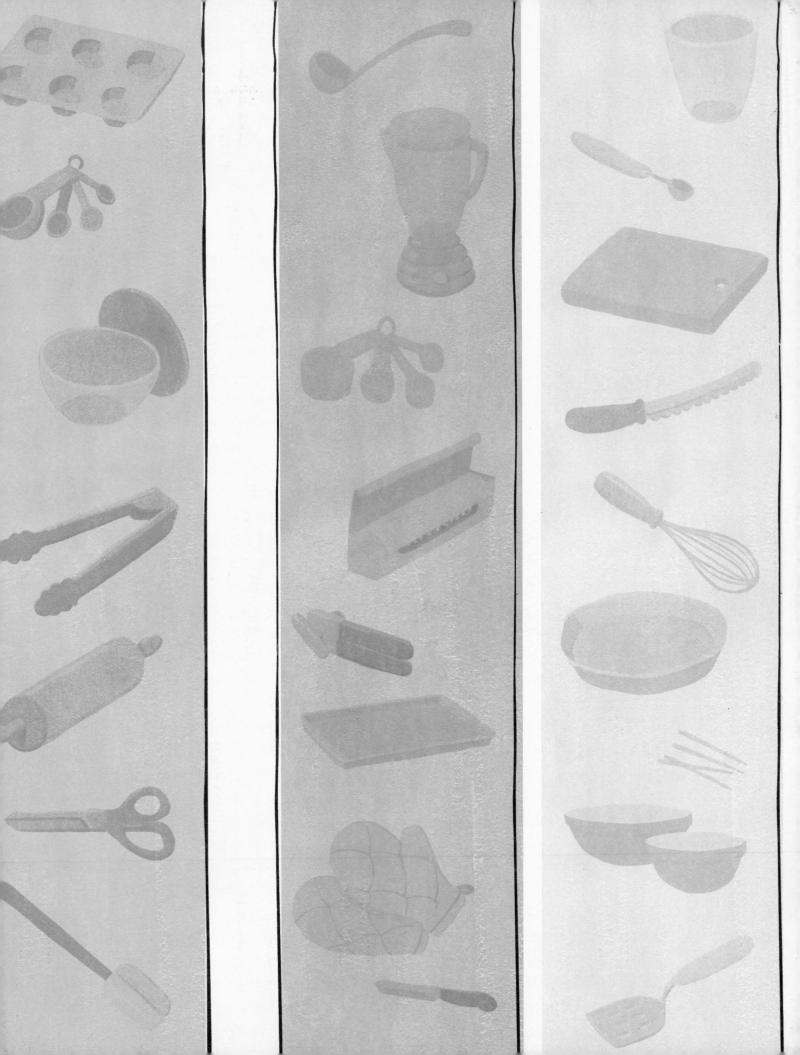

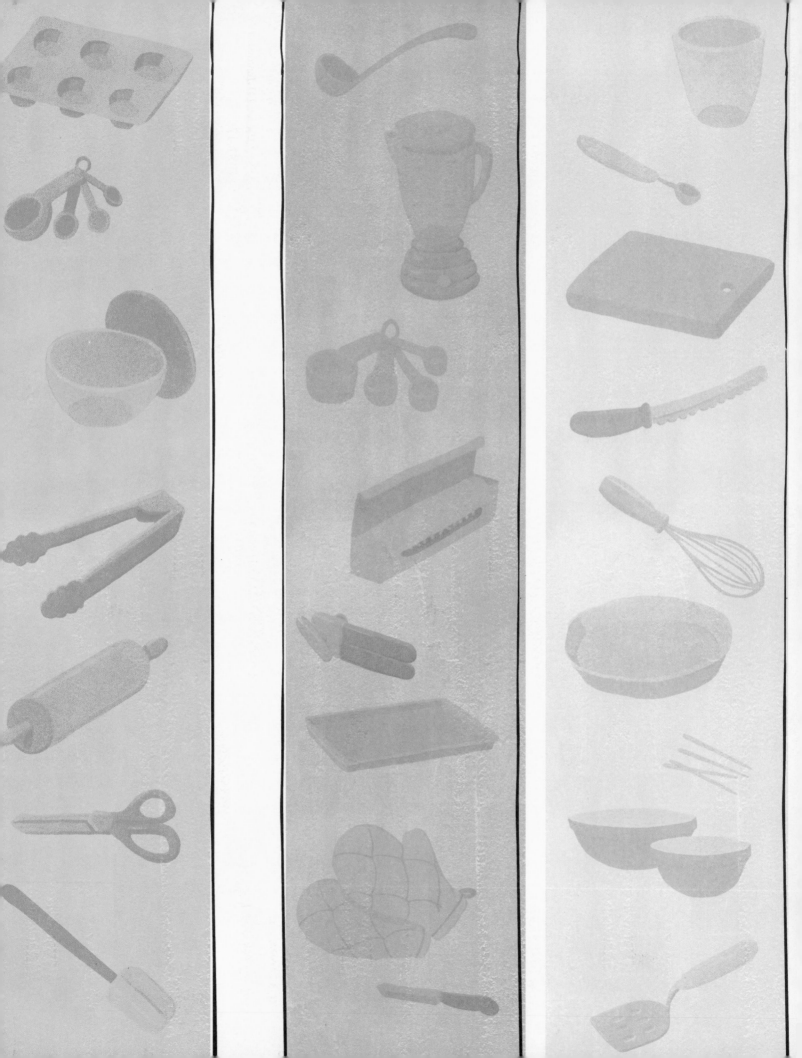